Pebble® Bilingüe/Bilingual Plus

Cómo hacer un
globo con olor misterioso
How to Make a
Mystery Smell Balloon

A divertirse con la ciencia

Hands-On Science Fun

por/by Lori Shores

Editora consultora/Consulting Editor: Gail Saunders-Smith, PhD

Consultor/Consultant: Ronald Browne, PhD
Departamento de Educación Elemental y de Primera Infancia/
Department of Elementary & Early Childhood Education
Universidad Estatal de Minnesota, Mankato/Minnesota State University, Mankato

CAPSTONE PRESS
a capstone imprint

Pebble Plus is published by Capstone Press,
151 Good Counsel Drive, P.O. Box 669, Mankato, Minnesota 56002.
www.capstonepub.com

Books published by Capstone Press are manufactured with paper
containing at least 10 percent post-consumer waste.

Library of Congress Cataloging-in-Publication Data
Shores, Lori.
  [How to make a mystery secret smell balloon. Spanish & English]
  Cómo hacer un globo con olor misterioso = How to make a mystery smell balloon / por Lori Shores.
      p. cm.—(Pebble plus bilingüe. A divertirse con la ciencia = Pebble plus bilingual. Hands-on science fun)
  Summary: "Simple text and full-color photos instruct readers how to make a mystery smell balloon and explains the
science behind the activity—in both English and Spanish"—Provided by publisher.
  Includes index.
  ISBN 978-1-4296-6108-9 (library binding)
  1. Science—Experiments—Juvenile literature. I. Title. II. Title: How to make a mystery smell balloon. III. Series.
Q164.S49718 2011
507.8—dc22   2010042262

Editorial Credits

Jenny Marks, editor; Strictly Spanish, translation services; Juliette Peters, designer; Danielle Ceminsky, bilingual book
    designer; Sarah Schuette; photo shoot direction; Marcy Morin, scheduler; Laura Manthe, production specialist

Photo Credits

Capstone Studio/Karon Dubke, all

Safety Note/Nota de seguridad

Please ask an adult for help in making your mystery smell balloon./
Pídele a un adulto que te ayude a hacer tu globo con olor misterioso.

Note to Parents and Teachers

The A divertirse con la ciencia/Hands-On Science Fun set supports national science standards
related to physical science. This book describes and illustrates making a mystery smell balloon
in both English and Spanish. The images support early readers in understanding the text. The
repetition of words and phrases helps early readers learn new words. This book also introduces
early readers to subject-specific vocabulary words, which are defined in the Glossary section.
Early readers may need assistance to read some words and to use the Table of Contents,
Glossary, Internet Sites, and Index sections of the book.

Printed in the United States of America in North Mankato, Minnesota.
092010   005933CGS11

Table of Contents

Tabla de contenidos

Getting Started

What's that smell?
Only you will know that it's a
mystery smell balloon. Your friends
won't believe their noses!

Para empezar

¿Qué es ese olor?
Sólo tú sabrás que es un globo
con olor misterioso. ¡Tus amigos
no podrán creer lo que huelen!

Here's what you need/Necesitarás:

1 latex balloon/
1 globo de látex

fork/tenedor

1 clove of garlic/
1 diente de ajo

ribbon or string/
cinta o cordel

small funnel/
embudo pequeño

Other smells to try/
Otros olores que puedes probar:

1 teaspoon (5 mL) vanilla extract/
1 cucharadita (5 ml) de extracto de vainilla
1 teaspoon (5 mL) pickle juice/
1 cucharadita (5 ml) de jugo de pepinillos
crushed onion/cebolla triturada

Making the Secret Smell

Peel the skin off the clove of garlic.

Crush the clove with the fork.
The garlic will be squished and juicy.

Cómo hacer el olor misterioso

Pela el diente de ajo.

Tritura el ajo con el tenedor.
El ajo quedará aplastado y jugoso.

6

Slide the small end
of the funnel in the
opening of the balloon.

Carefully dump the wet
garlic down the funnel.

Desliza el extremo pequeño del
embudo en la apertura del globo.

Introduce cuidadosamente el ajo
húmedo por el embudo.

Next, blow up the balloon
as big as you can.

Tie the end of the balloon
and shake it around.

A continuación, infla el globo tanto
como puedas.

Ata el extremo del globo y agítalo.

Sneak into a crowded room.
Tie the balloon to a chair or doorknob
using a ribbon. Now watch as
your friends notice the smell!

Entra silenciosamente a una habitación
donde haya mucha gente. Ata el globo a
una silla o a la perilla de una puerta
usando una cinta. ¡Ahora observa lo que
ocurre cuando tus amigos notan el olor!

How Does It Work?

Smelly things give off tiny pieces called molecules. They are too small to see. You smell garlic when the molecules reach your nose.

¿Cómo funciona?

Las cosas de olor fuerte desprenden pequeños pedazos llamados moléculas. Son demasiado pequeñas para verlas. Percibes el olor del ajo cuando la molécula llega a tu nariz.

Garlic molecules
pass through tiny holes
in the balloon.

Las moléculas de ajo
pasan por pequeños
agujeritos en el globo.

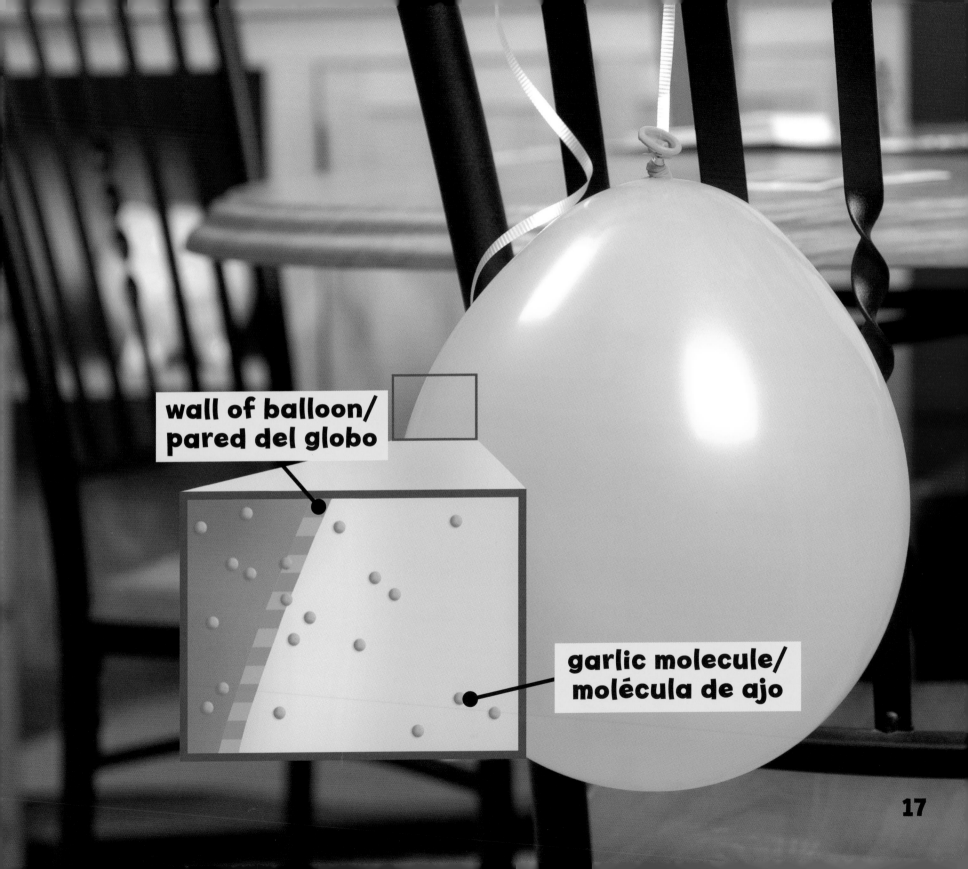

wall of balloon/
pared del globo

garlic molecule/
molécula de ajo

17

Air molecules are bigger. They can't pass through the holes as easily. Air stays in the balloon longer than the garlic molecules.

Las moléculas de aire son más grandes. No pueden pasar por los agujeros tan fácilmente. El aire se queda en el globo más tiempo que las moléculas de ajo.

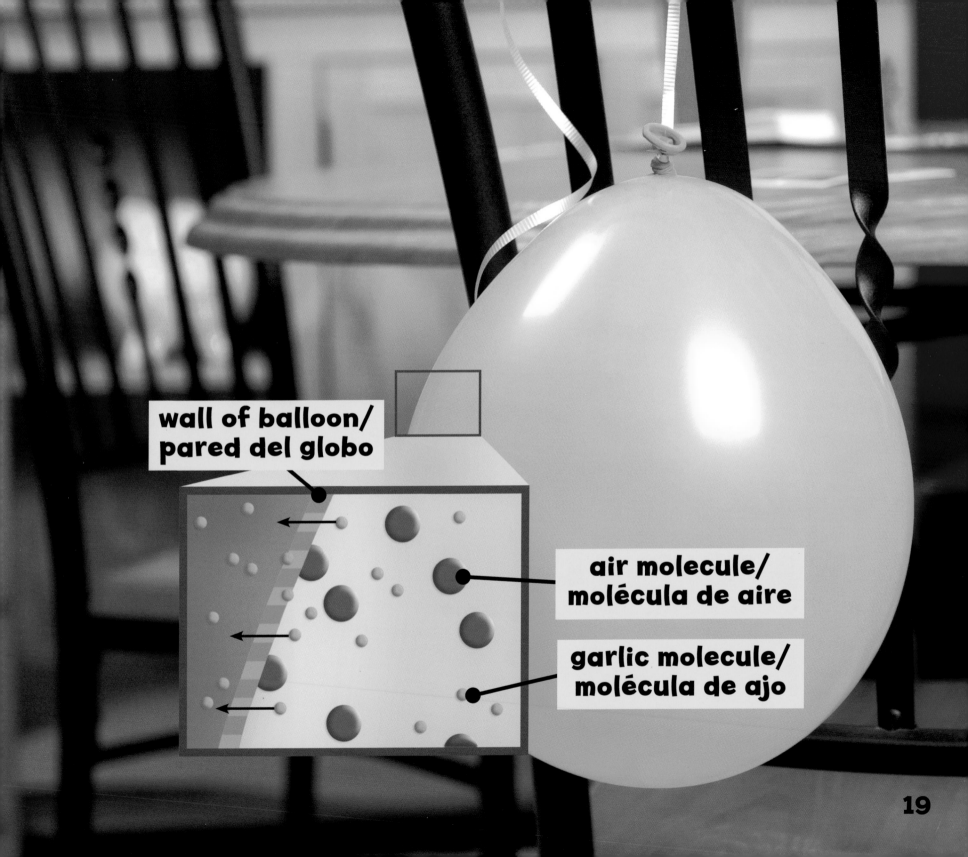

wall of balloon/
pared del globo

air molecule/
molécula de aire

garlic molecule/
molécula de ajo

19

The tiny garlic molecules
spread through the air.
Your friends crinkle their noses
as they sniff the molecules.

Las pequeñas moléculas de ajo se
diseminan por el aire.
Tus amigos arrugan la nariz
cuando huelen las moléculas.

Glossary

clove—one of the sections of a bulb of garlic

crinkle—to wrinkle up

funnel—an open cone that narrows to a tube

molecule—the smallest part of an element that can exist and still keep the characteristics of the element

peel—to remove the outer skin

Internet Sites

FactHound offers a safe, fun way to find Internet sites related to this book. All of the sites on FactHound have been researched by our staff.

Here's all you do:

Visit *www.facthound.com*

Type in this code: 9781429661089

 **Super-cool stuff!** Check out projects, games and lots more at www.capstonekids.com

Glosario

arrugar—encoger

el diente—una de las secciones de una cabeza de ajo

el embudo—un cono abierto que se hace estrecho hasta formar un tubo

la molécula—la parte más pequeña de un elemento que puede existir y seguir manteniendo las características del elemento

pelar—quitar la piel exterior

Sitios de Internet

FactHound brinda una forma segura y divertida de encontrar sitios de Internet relacionados con este libro. Todos los sitios en FactHound han sido investigados por nuestro personal.

Esto es todo lo que tienes que hacer:

Visita *www.facthound.com*

Ingresa este código: 9781429661089

¡Algo súper divertido! Hay proyectos, juegos y mucho más en www.capstonekids.com

Index

Índice